Date: 3/2/16

J 595.789 HAN
Hansen, Grace,
Butterflies /

PALM BEACH COUNTY
LIBRARY SYSTEM
3650 Summit Boulevard
West Palm Beach, FL 33406-4198

Butterflies

by Grace Hansen

Visit us at www.abdopublishing.com

Published by Abdo Kids, a division of ABDO, P.O. Box 398166, Minneapolis, Minnesota 55439.

Copyright © 2015 by Abdo Consulting Group, Inc. International copyrights reserved in all countries. No part of this book may be reproduced in any form without written permission from the publisher.

Printed in the United States of America, North Mankato, Minnesota.

032014

092014

 PRINTED ON RECYCLED PAPER

Photo Credits: iStock, Shutterstock, Thinkstock

Production Contributors: Teddy Borth, Jennie Forsberg, Grace Hansen

Design Contributors: Dorothy Toth, Renée LaViolette, Laura Rask

Library of Congress Control Number: 2013952076

Cataloging-in-Publication Data

Hansen, Grace.

 Butterflies / Grace Hansen.

   p. cm. -- (Insects)

ISBN 978-1-62970-039-7 (lib. bdg.)

Includes bibliographical references and index.

1. Butterflies--Juvenile literature.   I. Title.

595.78--dc23

                    2013952076

Table of Contents

Butterflies

Butterflies are insects. Beetles, dragonflies, and ants are all insects too.

All butterflies were once caterpillars. A caterpillar forms a **chrysalis**. It is like a shell.

7

A lot of changes happen inside.

Now it is an adult butterfly!

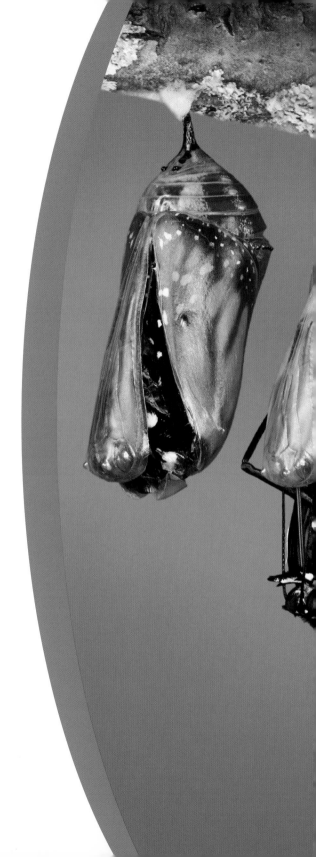

9

Butterflies live in many places.

You will often find them near

flowers and plants.

11

Butterflies come in all sizes and colors. Some butterflies have beautiful **patterns** on their wings.

Butterflies have three main body parts. They are the head, **thorax**, and the **abdomen**.

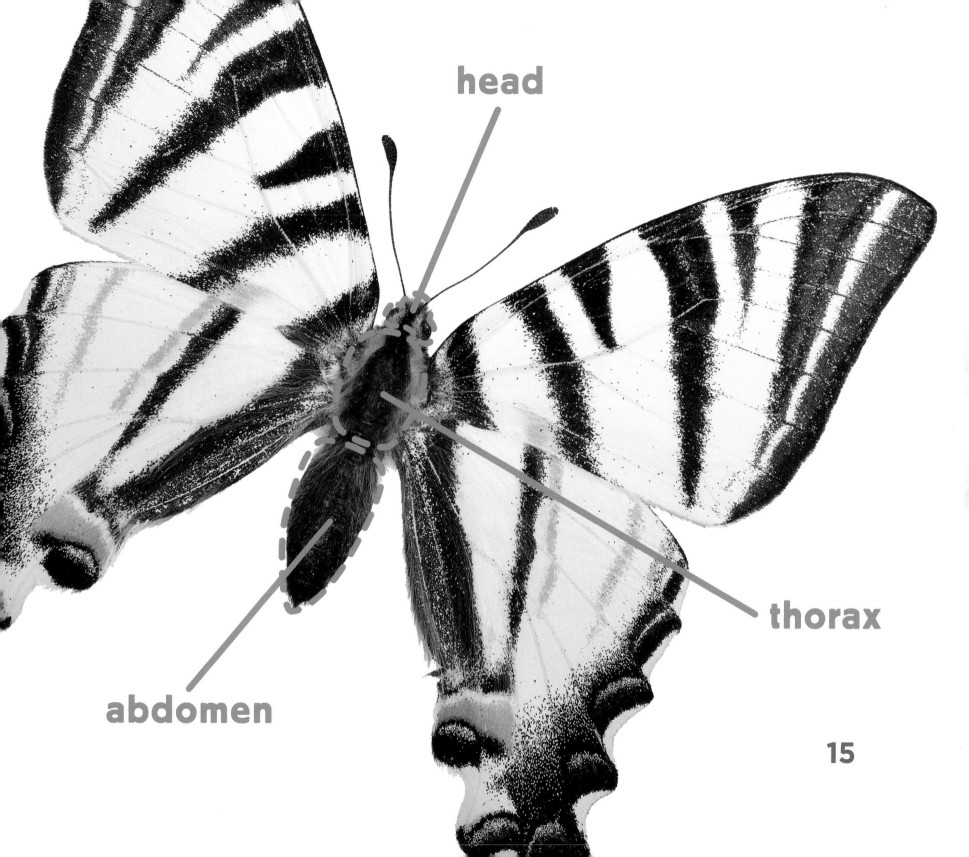

head

thorax

abdomen

15

Butterflies have two large eyes and two **antennae**. They have six legs and four wings.

Food

Butterflies drink **nectar**
and plant juices.

18

Butterflies Help the Earth

A butterfly moves **pollen** from flower to flower. This helps plants to grow.

21

More Facts

- North American monarch butterflies migrate 2,000 miles (3,219 km) in the fall and spring. They journey from the Great Lakes to the Gulf of Mexico.

- Butterflies can taste with their feet. When they land on a leaf or plant, they will know whether or not it is what they were looking for.

- Butterflies have a special mouthpart called a proboscis. It looks like a straw. They use it to drink **nectar** from plants.

Glossary

abdomen – the back part of an insect's body.

antennae – the two long, thin "feelers" on an insect's head.

caterpillar – a butterfly larva. It looks like a worm.

chrysalis – a hard shell encasing a butterfly in the pupal stage.

nectar – a sweet liquid, or sugar water, that flowering plants make.

pattern – a regular marking.

pollen – the tiny, yellow grains of flowers.

thorax – the middle part of an insect's body.

Index

abdokids.com

Use this code to log on to abdokids.com and access crafts, games, videos and more!

Abdo Kids Code:
IBK0397